Meet MAYA Cat

A story about acceptance.

WRITTEN BY: Lauren Beader

ILLUSTRATED BY: Harrison Makofsky

ART DIRECTED BY: Jillian Pacheco

International Standard Book Number
ISBN-13: 978-1727320596
ISBN-10: 172732059X

First edition.

THIS BOOK IS DEDICATED TO

Maya, who taught us a whole new kind of love. It's also dedicated to The Odd Cat Sanctuary because without them, Maya would not be here with us today. And to the Yellow Jackets Gymnastics Special Olympics team, who inspired me so many years ago and continue to surprise and inspire me today.

All proceeds will be donated The Odd Cat Sanctuary and to Special Olympics Massachusetts.

Meet
MAYA.

She's a
CAT.

She may look
A LITTLE DIFFERENT,

and she does need a little extra
ATTENTION SOMETIMES,

but she's just like
ANY OTHER CAT!

She likes to RUN AROUND.

She likes to
CLIMB ON THINGS.

She likes to PLAY WITH TOYS.

She likes to EAT YUMMY TREATS.

And she likes to talk.
A LOT.

When she's tired from
DOING ALL THAT,

she likes to sleep in
FLUFFY BLANKETS

AND CUDDLE
with her family.

MAYA MAY BE DIFFERENT,

She's not really that
DIFFERENT AT ALL!

She likes to be treated and loved just like **EVERYBODY ELSE.**

Thanks for taking the time to read Maya's story!

We hope it helps you see that everyone deserves love and acceptance.

This book is based on the story of a wonderfully real cat, really named Maya. To learn more about Maya, check out her Instagram page @meetmayacat.

We are truly grateful to The Odd Cat Sanctuary in Salem, MA. They saved Maya's life, just like they save so many other cats every single day. They deserve all the support they can get. To learn more about The Odd Cat Sanctuary, find them on Facebook.

And we offer our full support to Special Olympics, an organization that provides free athletics programs to children and adults with intellectual disabilities in all 50 states and 172 countries globally. Within Massachusetts alone, Special Olympics works with 12,500 children and adults all across the state, holding nearly 300 sporting events each year. These programs not only improve athletic and social skills, but also build confidence and encourage inclusion. Learn more at specialolympicsma.org.

Made in the USA
Middletown, DE
05 November 2018